SMARTER BRANDING

Without Breaking The Bank

Five Proven Marketing Strategies You Can Use Right Now
to Build Your Business at Little or No Cost

Brenda Bence

INTERNATIONAL BRANDING EXPERT AND COACH

Global Insight

TABLE OF CONTENTS

What is "Good" Marketing?
The Good, The Bad ... and The Ugly

Paperback: Chapter 1, page 20   *Video: Session #2, time 06:16* [*]

Action: Be alert and keep a look-out for examples of what you consider to be "good" marketing ... leaf through magazines, surf the net, check out billboards, watch television — look anywhere where you will find marketing communications.

Based on those examples, what do *you* think makes up genuinely good marketing? Share your examples and your findings here.

Example: **Why it qualifies as *good* marketing:**

_____   _____

_____   _____

_____   _____

You can learn as much from "bad" marketing as you can from "good" marketing ... after all, it teaches you what *not* to do, how *not* to communicate effectively.

As you were looking for good marketing examples, what "bad" communication efforts did you find? What did they teach you? Share your examples and your findings here:

Example: **Why it represents *bad* marketing:**

_____   _____

_____   _____

_____   _____

Summarize: Based on your findings, what adjectives would you use to describe truly "good" marketing? List them here.

_____

_____

[*] *Video times are approximate and may vary depending upon viewing software.*

THE PAPERCLIP CHALLENGE:
THE WISDOM OF A PAPERCLIP

Paperback: Chapter 1, page 22   *Video: Session #2, time 10:10*

Action: Set a typical paperclip in front of you and look at it carefully while asking yourself the following question:

"What are all the things I *cannot* do with this paperclip?"

Your task is to make the longest list possible within three minutes.

Caution: Challenge every possible answer you come up with! For example, if you say, "I cannot *write* with a paperclip," I would disagree. You could easily open up a paper clip, dip the tip of the paperclip into an ink well, and use it to write. Another example: If you said "I cannot *eat* a paperclip," I would reply, "Sure you can!" You could cut it up into little pieces, sprinkle it onto your salad, and eat to your heart's delight. (You'd be crazy if you did so, but nonetheless, it's possible!) So, again, challenge each and every answer you come up with.

List of things you cannot do with a paperclip: (Remember — you only have three minutes!)

_____

_____

_____

_____

_____

_____

_____

_____

At the end of this exercise, most people find they can do more with a paperclip than they ever imagined! It's the same with your company's existing assets — you can do more with them than you think.

IDEAS AND ACTION STEPS TEMPLATE

Video: Session #3, time 00:56 (and referred to throughout the video program)

Ideas	Action Steps

TARGET GROUP & NEEDS EXERCISE:
TAKE AIM AT YOUR TARGET!

Paperback:
Chapter 5, page 47
Chapter 6, page 54

Video:
Session #6, time 07:36
Session #7, time 12:30

Customer Type (Demographics / Psychographics / Attitudes): _____

_____

_____

_____

_____

Who Currently Use / Buy ... (Current Usage / Behaviors): _____

_____

_____

_____

_____

And Who Need (Functional / Physical and/or Emotional Needs): _____

_____

_____

_____

_____

COMPETITIVE FRAMEWORK EXERCISE:
YOUR BRAND'S SECRET IDENTITY

Paperback: Chapter 7, page 61   *Video: Session #8, time 13:48*

Standard Identity

The Standard Identity of my business is _____.

When I think of my business only in these terms, my competitors are _____

_____

_____

_____.

Perceptual Competitive Framework*

If I could get my target customers to think of my business as _____

_____,

then my competitive set would expand to include _____

_____

_____

_____,

and I would have a much greater source of business potential.

REMEMBER:

When is an apple not an apple?

* Concept of Brand Development Network International

WHAT ARE YOUR BRAND BENEFITS?
SERVE YOUR CUSTOMERS A SILVER PLATTER

Paperback: Chapter 8, page 67   *Video: Session #9, time 10:43*

1. What are the unique promises you want to — and can — own with your brand?

Possible FUNCTIONAL Benefits   Possible EMOTIONAL Benefits

_____   _____

_____   _____

_____   _____

_____   _____

_____   _____

_____   _____

2. Input Your Customers' Needs Here
   (see "Target Group" Exercise)

Functional:

_____

_____

_____

Emotional:

_____

_____

_____

3. List Here the Final Top one, two or three
   Most Desired Benefits For Your Brand

Functional
Emotional

REASONS WHY WORKSHEET: PROVE IT!

Paperback: Chapter 9, page 76   *Video: Session #10, time 14:15*

1. List your final one to three key brand Benefits in the left column.

2. Now, in the right column, list out your final, strongest Reasons Why to support these Benefits (after you've completed the Reason-Why Thought Starter).

3. Be sure to confirm that the Benefits and Reasons Why link; do you have Reasons Why to support each one of your Benefits?

Benefits		**Reasons Why**
• _____	→	• _____
_____		_____
_____		_____
_____		_____
• _____	→	• _____
_____		_____
_____		_____
_____		_____
• _____	→	• _____
_____		_____
_____		_____
_____		_____

REASONS WHY THOUGHT STARTER:
WHY, OH WHY, SHOULD THEY BUY?

Paperback: Chapter 9, page 76   *Video: Session #10, time 15:06*

1. List your final Brand Benefit(s) here: _____

    _____

    _____

2. Now, which of the types of Reasons Why listed below could you use to support your Brand Benefit(s)?

    Design? _____

    _____

    Ingredients? _____

    _____

    Endorsement? _____

    _____

    Process? _____

    _____

    Product or Service Attributes / Features? _____

    _____

    Source? _____

    _____

    Background / Education? _____

    _____

    Accreditation / Certifications? _____

    _____

    Awards? _____

    _____

    Other? _____

    _____

BENEFITS & REASONS WHY WORKSHEET

Paperback: Chapter 9, page 75   *Video: Session #10, time 16:45*

- Are your brand's Benefits Functional / Rational? Emotional? Both?

- What is the *promise* your brand is making to your Customer that is unique to you / your brand? Or, that your brand can deliver in a unique way?

- Why should your Customer believe your brand can deliver that promise?

Benefits	Reasons Why
• _____ →	• _____

BRAND CHARACTER EXPLORATION:
DO THE 'MAGAZINE SHUFFLE'

Paperback: Chapter 10, page 81   *Video: Session #11, time 09:35*

To stimulate your creative juices and get you thinking about your own Brand Character, grab some magazines and sit down with your favorite cup of coffee or tea (or something stronger, if you think it would help!) Leaf through the pages of the magazines, looking for two different types of visuals:

- Visuals that you think *do* represent the Brand Character of your brand.

- Visuals that you *don't* think represent the Brand Character of your brand.

Remember: It's just as important to know what you *don't* want to stand for as it is to know what you *do* want to stand for.

Description of pictures that do represent my Brand Character:

_____

_____

_____

_____

What adjectives come to mind when looking at this visual?

_____

_____

_____

_____

Description of pictures that don't represent my brand character:

_____

_____

_____

_____

Why not?

_____

_____

_____

_____

BRAND CHARACTER THOUGHT STARTER:
WHAT'S YOUR BRAND'S "PERSONALITY?"

Paperback: Chapter 10, page 80   *Video: Session #11, time 09:58*

To further your thinking about possible words that might describe your desired Brand Character, below is a sample list of adjectives. Are there any here that you think are consistent with the character of *your* brand? Circle those that you think best describe your brand, then underline those words that you believe *least* describe your brand. Remember: Knowing what your brand character "isn't" is just as important as knowing what your brand character "is."

Irreverent	Serene	Dedicated
Rascal	Earnest	Even-tempered
Street-wise	Sparkling	Decisive
Authentic	Soulful	Vivacious
Maverick	Eloquent	Generous
Seasoned	Soft-spoken	Chic
Focused	Gregarious	Spiritual
Gracious	Grounded	Considerate
Altruistic	Industrious	Sociable
Fair-minded	Courageous	Visionary
Colorful	Approachable	Daring
Magnetic	Whimsical	Ethical
Inspirational	Direct	Exotic
Engaging	Wise	Encouraging
Influential	Persuasive	Passionate

Did any additional, better brand character descriptors pop into your mind as you were doing this exercise? If so, write them here.

_____

_____

_____

_____

_____

_____

Brand Character Worksheet:
Make Sure Your Brand Isn't Bland!

Paperback: Chapter 10, page 80   *Video: Session #11, time 10:14*

Based on the various Brand Character tools we've discussed, list out here all of the adjectives that you believe describe the character of your brand. Get creative! Don't go for normal words ('caring, approachable, professional'). Instead, try to find words that are unique and ownable.

_____

_____

_____

_____

Sometimes, a 'narrative descriptor' works best to describe your brand's character — a brief sentence that talks about the character of your brand as though it were a person. Give it a try, below, and once again, don't go for the "standard" approach (e.g., 'trusted leader who cares about his customers' — yawn …). Think outside the box, and see what you can come up with.

_____

_____

_____

_____

Now, take a fresh look at both your list of adjectives and your narrative descriptor, and ask yourself:

"Will my specific Target Group find these attributes appealing?"

This is critical because, if your brand's character doesn't appeal to your target, your brand simply won't be successful. Make adjustments as needed based on this assessment, and fill in your final Brand Character below.

My Final Brand Character:

_____

_____

Brand Positioning Statement Template

Paperback: Chapter 11, page 83   Video: Session #11, time 02:58 and 11:18

TO *(Target Group):*

- *Demographics, Psychographics, Attitudes*

- *Current Usage & Behaviors*

- *Needs (Functional / Emotional)*

(BRAND NAME) _____

IS THE BRAND OF *(Competitive Framework):* _____

_____

(Competing mainly with) _____

_____

THAT PROVIDES *(Benefits):* _____

_____

_____

BECAUSE *(Reasons Why):*

1. _____

2. _____

3. _____

THE BRAND CHARACTER IS:
(Descriptors and/or Narrative) _____

_____

_____

INFERRED BRAND POSITIONING STATEMENT: *CALIFORNIA WOW!*

Paperback: Chapter 11, page 84   *Video: Session #12, time 05:34*

TO *(Target Group):*

- *Demographics, Psychographics, Attitudes*
  Urban 'social' and single adults, aged 18-29, who are 'in the know' about all that is going on, trendy and fashionable. Their work is important to them, but their social life is truly pivotal to the quality of their lives, and to stay in touch with others, they talk on the phone, SMS, e-mail, and blog regularly. They love to be surrounded by music and use iPods while walking on the street, taking the subway. They eat out with friends on weekends, go to movies, and go clubbing where they enjoy dancing, meeting others, and checking out fashions. They want to be in healthy shape physically because they know it's good for you and they want to look great in whatever they're wearing, too, so they try to exercise whenever they can. But, to enjoy exercise, it needs to be inexpensive and fun, and that means having friends and other social people around to make the experience full of enjoyment.

- *Current Usage & Behaviors*
  They don't exercise all that much right now, but they know they should, not only for health but because regular exercise will help keep them looking good. Right now, they get most of their exercise by walking and when they go out dancing & clubbing with friends.

- *Needs (Rational / Emotional)*
  An inexpensive, 'hip' fitness club where they can get a great workout, can see and be seen, have fun, and meet new friends in the process.

(BRAND NAME) California WOW Fitness Center

IS THE BRAND OF *(Competitive Framework):* Hip & Fun Workout Experience

(Competitive mainly with): Dancing, clubbing, other fitness facilities.

THAT PROVIDES *(Benefits):* The city's most fun, hip, and social exercise facility at a good value.

BECAUSE *(Reasons Why):*

1. State of the art fitness equipment in 48,000 square feet of space
2. Eight different club locations with interchangeable membership
3. Fun Start / Fit Start program
4. Membership available for as low as $20 per month
5. Energetic, beautiful personal trainers who are not only well trained, but who make exercising fun, too
6. The fitness center that the most television celebrities and models belong to
7. Offer fun, group exercise alternatives such as Punch! Kick! Jump! classes.
8. Energetic music piped throughout the club all day and all night long

THE BRAND CHARACTER IS:

(Descriptors and/or Narrative) Trendy, fun, outgoing, and social. The kind of person you love to go clubbing with. In great shape, popular, and good looking, too. Aspirational.

Inferred Brand Positioning Statement: *Cascade Club*

Paperback: Chapter 11, page 86   *Video: Session #12, time 08:08*

TO *(Target Group):*

- *Demographics, Psychographics, Attitudes*
  Downtown-based successful working professionals, aged 35–55, whose career pressures, long work days, and busy travel schedules leave them little free time for exercise. They strive to be the best and to surround themselves with the best in all they do. Their career successes have led them to become increasingly accustomed to the finer things in life. They understand and appreciate the importance of remaining healthy, and they know that regular exercise and maintaining a healthy life style is critical to their continued success in life.

- *Current Usage & Behaviors*
  They may have access to fitness equipment either in their homes or in the workplace, and they try to fit as much exercise into their schedules as they can. But it's extremely difficult to find the time, and at the end of a long work day, they often find themselves too tired to exercise. If they exercise at work or at home, they are often "torn" — reminded of responsibilities when they see colleagues and/or their families. If they commit to, and spend good money on, joining a fitness club, they will use it.

- *Needs (Rational / Emotional)*
  They seek a top-of-the-line exercise and health club where they can get away from the pressures of their work and personal lives and focus on themselves for a while. They want the very best machines, personal trainers, and workout facilities in the city in a luxurious "pampering" environment.

(BRAND NAME) Cascade Club

IS THE BRAND OF *(Competitive Framework):* Private health and lifestyle oasis.

(Competing mainly with:) 5-star hotel fitness clubs and spas, Fitness First, other private clubs, independent top-end spas.

THAT PROVIDES *(Benefits):* The city's best overall health, exercise, and lifestyle facility where you can achieve your health goals and pamper yourself in private club luxury.

BECAUSE *(Reasons Why):*

1. State-of-the-art exercise equipment in 3,500 square meters of pristine training and fitness rooms

2. Best certified personal trainers in the country for individualized goal attainment

3. Full range of health, beauty, and lifestyle amenities (luxurious changing rooms, separate male and female saunas, steam and Jacuzzi rooms, accompanying spa, private poolside cabanas, wine and juice bar, and poolside dining options)

THE BRAND CHARACTER IS:

(Descriptors and/or Narrative) Prestigious, exclusive, premium, luxurious. A perfectionist who desires the very best. Service-minded and supportive — a life coach who understands your needs and who will help you achieve your fitness and personal goals.

How to Tackle Social Media: Get Back to the Basics

Paperback: Chapter 12, page 93   *Video: Session #13, time 09:23*

In the last few years, the excitement of social media has been keeping marketers, branders, and business owners up at night. As they explore this relatively new, uncharted territory, business managers all across the globe are asking themselves questions they never would have conceived of just ten years ago. "What's our Facebook strategy for driving customer loyalty?" "Who should be managing our brand's Twitter account?" "How do we leverage YouTube to create the next big 'talk-of-the-globe' video?"

Social media has become the Goliath to every marketer's David. In case you've been sleeping at the wheel, here are a few facts for perspective:

- The number of people on Facebook is now far larger than some of the most populous nations. Indeed, at the time of this writing, if Facebook were a country, it would be the third largest in the world.

- At one point in time, Twitter was doubling its population every 90 days and now reportedly has almost 200 million monthly visits.

- More than 25% of all web searches end up at YouTube, making it the second largest search engine in the world.

Rupert Murdoch, the publishing magnate, is quoted as saying that these changes represent the biggest shift in communications since the invention of the printing press 500 years ago. So, clearly, social media is not a fad. It's here to stay, and it is fundamentally changing not only the way we communicate with customers, but the way customers communicate with each other.

The Fundamentals Haven't Changed

But in the midst of all this flurry of excitement, it's important for business leaders to sit back, take a deep breath, and remember: "How" we communicate with clients may be changing dramatically, but "what" we communicate should not change.

In truth, the means we use to communicate with our customers has changed many times over the years (remember how excited advertisers originally were about television?), but the *essence* of brand building hasn't changed in decades: Know your target audience intimately, dig deep to understand the target's functional and emotional needs, and make sure your brand responds to those needs better than the competition. By doing this, you gain loyal brand users. Then, never ever give those loyal consumers a reason to switch to another brand.

It's really that simple.

Relationships — A Constant

The buzz word I hear more and more these days when it comes to social media is "relationship." "We must build a *relationship* with our customers using social media!" cry the marketers. But building a relationship between your brand and your customers has *always* been at the core of good brand building. That hasn't changed. *How* you choose to build that relationship is what is evolving. Building relationships is something marketers should be doing day in and day out.

If anything, the onslaught of new social media outlets has made building a relationship with your target market not only easier but, frankly, less expensive, too. After all, we don't need to lay down thousands of dollars to send out regular tweets! But the fundamental nature of your brand's relationship with customers hasn't changed at all. It's still about delighting your consumers every single time they come in touch with your brand.

With so much new media terrain to explore, there's never been a more exciting time to be managing a brand. Facebook, Twitter, YouTube, and other social media sites are all great tools to further your brand's positioning in the marketplace. Just don't let the excitement of that steer you away from the true essence of brand building. Stick with the basics, and you can't go wrong.

> " *... Building a relationship between your brand and your customers has **always** been at the core of good brand building. That hasn't changed. **How** you choose to build that brand is what is changing ...* "

Positioning Wheel Template

Paperback: Chapter 12, page 97   *Video: Session #13, time 13:41*

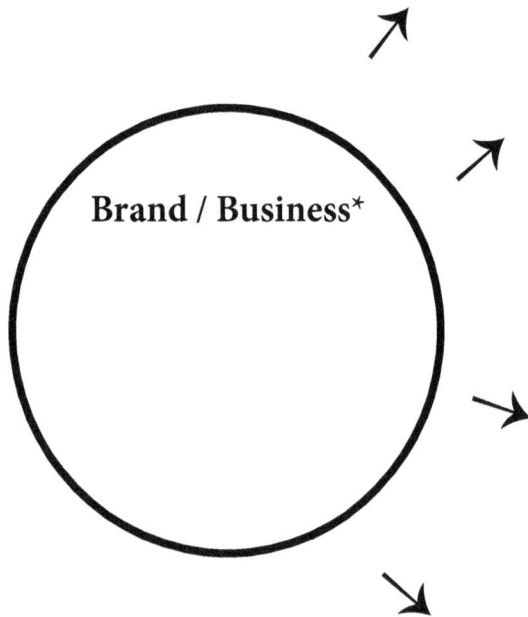

Positioning Activity #1: _____

- _____

- _____

Brand / Business*

Positioning Activity #2: _____

- _____

- _____

Positioning Activity #3: _____

- _____

- _____

Positioning Activity #4: _____

- _____

- _____

* Write your brief positioning overview statement here.

DISCOVERING CURRENT UNMET CUSTOMER NEEDS

Paperback: Chapter 13, page 99   *Video: Session #14, time 17:00*

When it comes to brainstorming to uncover current unmet needs of your customers, you can definitely do it by yourself, if need be. But, this is one of those situations where the more minds you have working together, the better results you are likely to get.

So, I encourage you to enlist some folks to help you with this. Consider people in your business who deal with customers most closely and/or people who know well what you currently have to offer. Or, maybe you can enlist the smartest business person you know to brainstorm along with you. The key is to get as many minds as you can working on uncovering these unmet customer needs that are so critical to the development of your business and your brand.

Remember to include emotional needs, too! Listen carefully for when a customer says, "I feel …" That's a sure-fire sign that you're uncovering emotional needs.

Possible Current Unmet Needs of Customers:

_____

_____

_____

_____

_____

_____

_____

_____

_____

_____

Once you have a complete list, go back and circle those that you think could provide the biggest opportunities for your brand. Conduct a focus group with potential and existing customers or run an online survey to confirm customers' level of interest.

Discovering *New* Customer Needs

Paperback: Chapter 13, page 99   *Video: Session #14, time 18:44*

Similar to brainstorming current *unmet* needs of your customers, you can focus on discovering *new* customer needs by yourself or — if possible — with a group. Ideas grow and morph when shared with others, so I encourage you to enlist a group of people and brainstorm together.

Just brainstorm for now — don't judge! — and come up with as many ideas as you can about what *new* customer needs exist out there for your existing and potential customers.

Possible NEW Customer Needs:

_____

_____

_____

_____

_____

_____

_____

_____

_____

_____

_____

Once you have a complete list, go back and circle those that you think could provide the biggest opportunities for your brand. Conduct a focus group with potential and existing customers or run an online survey to confirm the needs that have the most potential.

How to Uncover New Customer Needs: Treasure Chest of Ideas

Video: Session #14, time 22:40

Based on inputs from past *Smarter Branding* workshop participants from around the globe, below is a compiled list of some possible ways you can uncover *new* customer needs. Use this list as inspiration, then sit back and reflect … What else could you do — for your specific industry and business — to uncover even *more* customer needs?

Remember: Staying on top of customer needs is fundamental to successful brand building!

- Adapt successful ideas from other countries
- Ask colleagues about customer needs (if they know your Target Group well)
- Ask customers to take a survey
- Ask customers what they like/dislike about your competitors
- Ask industry analysts for input
- Ask open-ended questions, never "yes/no" questions
- Ask potential customers about their biggest problems or what is missing in their business/life
- Ask potential customers about their business plans and objectives
- Ask questions of close-but-not-exactly-on-target-group customers in order to find potential related needs
- Ask questions of people who know nothing about your business; get fresh perspective
- Ask your staff for input based on their observations
- Attend seminars in your potential customers' business segment
- Be at the places where your target customers congregate
- Brainstorm with your "non" marketing team — R&D, Sales, Finance, etc.
- Conduct a "new idea" contest — internally and/or externally
- Conduct in-home visits with potential customers
- Conduct in-store sampling, if appropriate
- Conduct seminars with various topics, and run surveys at the end
- Conduct street interviews, pin-pointing your target audience, if possible
- Create a game to make asking new customer opinions more fun
- Create an anonymous blog and invite comments
- Develop relationships with key managers at your client's site

(Treasure Chest of Ideas, continued)

- Go to customer's site and shadow them for one day — experience first-hand their biggest issues
- Go to industry nights/events to meet new customers and ask them questions
- Go to trade shows
- Hire a research agency
- Hold a meeting specifically to discuss a particular client's business
- Interrupt customers at stores to ask about needs and new trends
- Invite customers to your location for a tour
- Join a group with other non-competitive companies all targeting the same group of people — exchange ideas
- List your service or product on information portals and encourage people to comment about what they like and don't like about your industry
- Mail out confidential feedback forms
- Offer free gifts, trials, or samples in exchange for feedback
- Organize a "meet-the-expert session" where customers can ask questions
- Place an interactive booth in a store and staff it to ask questions to potential customers
- Plan a "day in the life of customers" — in their homes, in their offices, etc. wherever is appropriate. Spend the whole day with customers to understand their lifestyle.
- Questionnaires and surveys for potential customers
- Read publications that your customers read
- Read trade magazines to find out how customers' industries are changing
- Review forecasts for upcoming market trends
- Stay on top of recent regulatory changes — what impact will those have on your customers?
- Study the complaints of competitors' customers on the Internet
- Train your help desk staff to ask informative "new-need" questions
- Use ethnography — observe customers using your products and services (or those of your competitors) real-time
- Visit chat rooms on the Internet that your customers frequent
- Visit websites of potential customers to understand their businesses
- Volunteer to work at a customer's company for free for a day
- Watch for trends in databases/ online directories
- Watch the customer using competitive products
- Watch TV for new trends and ask customers how those trends will impact their business or their lives

Recognizing and Rewarding Customers

Paperback: Chapter 14, page 116   *Video: Session #15, time 07:51*

Either by yourself or with a team, brainstorm every possible way you can think to recognize and reward your customers. Get creative! If *you* were your customer, how would you like to be recognized? What kinds of recognition or rewards would be most meaningful to you? Which ones would stand out the most? What are your competitors doing to recognize and reward their customers? How could you do it better? List all ideas here.

_____

_____

_____

_____

_____

_____

_____

_____

_____

_____

_____

_____

_____

Now, grab a marker and highlight those which you feel would most make a customer feel recognized. Which ones are most consistent with your brand, what it stands for, and your brand character? Those are the ones you want to focus on.

RECOGNIZING AND REWARDING CUSTOMERS: TREASURE CHEST OF IDEAS

Video: Session #15, time 08:47

Below is a compilation of ideas to recognize and reward existing customers that have been shared in *Smarter Branding* workshops all around the world. You will see these ideas vary greatly, but they represent dozens of ways you can easily — and cheaply — recognize and reward your existing customers. Read through this for some stimulus, and then challenge yourself to come up with even more ideas. Remember: The key to growing a strong brand is to build strong relationships with your customers!

P.S. Did you come up with any other great ideas that you'd like to share? We'd love to hear them! Just send us an e-mail at Ideas@Smarter-Branding.com.

- Allow customers to buy products at special prices
- Allow customers to promote their business in some way through your business
- Always be on the look-out on your customers' behalf — share ideas for how they could make more money
- Always provide great service and apologize for any mistakes — redeem the mistake with a gift
- Arrange a special activity or event to entertain customers
- Ask customers their opinions on important business matters
- Be a sponsor for a customer's event
- Be sure you, your receptionist, and your staff greet customers by name
- Buy customers personalized gifts
- Conduct offsite meetings and sessions with valuable industry information and invite customers to attend
- Constantly innovate and improve your service
- Continue to treat existing clients as if they were new clients
- Continuously provide news/samples communicating new products to current consumers
- Contribute to customers' staff parties
- Create a "Best Customer" award or a "Customer of the Month" award to recognize your best customers
- Create a "Best Feedback Award" to reward customers for their inputs
- Create a frequent buyer/loyalty program
- Create a membership program and customize your products/services for members

(Treasure Chest of Ideas, continued)

- Create discounts/special packages/VIP cards for loyal customers

- Create special networking events just for top customers

- E-mail to customers any interesting on-line articles you find; let them know you are thinking of them

- Give a priority pass for the lounge at the airport

- Give certificates or freebies as a token of appreciation for the number of products purchased

- Give customers a behind-the-scenes tour of your site/office

- Give flowers to key customer's assistants on International Assistants' Day

- Give free gift vouchers to frequent customers

- Give graduation gifts to key clients' children

- Give memorable and strategic year-end presents

- Give movie tickets as a gift

- Give product previews to key customers (like sneak previews at the movie)

- Give recognition awards that can be published in local newspaper or online, e.g., on your website

- Go the extra mile, every time

- Have a VIP customer dinner party once a year

- Have your staff over to your house to bake cookies, then send the cookies to your best clients

- Help customers get publicized in appropriate media

- Help customers grow their businesses by recommending customers to others

- Help customers to review their own return-on-investment of their programs

- Hold a monthly gathering or party for those customers/clients who purchased the most that month

- Host a potluck dinner with your staff and theirs

- Invite customers to speak at your sales meeting or business meeting

- Invite important customers to your home for dinner — get to know customers more personally

- Invite loyal customers to company anniversary parties

- Make a donation to your customers' favorite charity in their name

- Make unexpected personal phone calls to key customers to express appreciation

- Nominate customers for awards

- Offer a free analysis of a customer's purchasing patterns

(Treasure Chest of Ideas, continued)

- Offer better ways to make it easy for regular customers to pay
- Offer customers nice incentives for referrals
- Offer financing to important customers
- Offer pre-order opportunities by phone or e-mail
- Offer special promotions at the end of the year only for customers who have purchased from you X times in those 365 days
- Offer to drive customers to the airport on their way out of town
- Offer to speak at customers' sales or business meeting
- Offer trainings, seminars, webinars exclusively for your key customers
- Offer unique products only for regular customers
- Offer volume discounts for multiple purchases
- Offer your own company shares at a discounted price
- Plan dinner/lunch meetings with customers at their favorite restaurants — let customers choose
- Plan events for a group of your clients' staff members
- Post customers' achievements on your website
- Profile customers in your newsletter or advertisements (with permission)
- Propose reciprocal partnerships with customers
- Provide a free consultant to customers
- Provide customers a great testimonial about what it's like to work with them
- Provide free appropriate publication subscriptions or whitepapers
- Provide free market information from the geographic areas where your customers are located
- Provide increasingly nice loyalty gifts for clients who have done business with you for two years, five years, 10 years …
- Recognize customers publicly with an award within their industry
- Refer business to customers regularly
- Remember small details and what's important to customers, e.g., their favorite drinks, food, habits, hobbies — keep a data base and review it every time you go to see that client
- Remember the first names of customer's staff members
- Remember the names of personal family members of key clients
- Run a contest for all customers, asking them to send in their ideas; the winning idea receives a prize

(Treasure Chest of Ideas, continued)

- Scour newspapers/online for topics related to customers' favorite subjects and forward customers the information — let customers know you are thinking of them

- Send a birthday cake to a customer's office once a month — intended for all customers' employees who have birthdays that month

- Send birthday and holiday cards

- Send congratulations notes on customers' successes

- Send handwritten thank you notes — for no reason other than to just say 'thank you'

- Set up a Google Alert for your customer's key competitors, then forward the information to your customer when it arrives in your inbox

- Set up a unique phone line only for your best customers

- Showcase a particular customer in your newsletter

- Sponsor client charity events

- Staff on site [in a store] remember customer's names and what kind of products they like

- Start a monthly 'lucky draw' for all customers who purchase XX amount

- Start a program of "buy one or more, get one free"

- Start an annual customer lucky draw for a free weekend away

- Take a client's family out to dinner with yours

- Take customers to their favorite sporting events

- Thank customers regularly and let customers know how much you value their business

- Throw a birthday party for a loyal customer

- Treat customers like family

- Use your frequent flyer points to upgrade a client's flight

- Visit them at their office — face to face — instead of phoning

- When on holiday, send customers a post card

- Write an informative newsletter with valuable tips

CUSTOMER BRAND REFERRALS WORKSHEET

Paperback: Chapter 14, page 118   *Video: Session #15, time 14:25*

Getting customer brand referrals through people who are already familiar with you and your business is a great way to build your brand — at little or no cost at all. After all, these people know and trust your existing brand so they are in the best position to talk to others knowledgeably about what you have to offer.

Use the space below to write down all the ways you could get more customer brand referrals. Think about how you have gotten brand referrals in the past … or how you have referred others in the past. What prompted those actions? List all ideas here.

_____

_____

_____

_____

_____

_____

_____

_____

_____

_____

_____

_____

Now, review your list. Which of these ideas would be most powerful? Circle the ones that you believe would get the best results.

How to Get More Brand Referrals: Treasure Chest of Ideas

Video: Session #15, time 15:07

Smarter Branding workshop participants have shared a variety of ideas about how to get more brand referrals. Which ideas would work well for you and your business? Brainstorm more once you've read through this list.

- Arrange a joint marketing event with other companies who all target the same group — refer each others' businesses

- Ask for referrals on the back of your business card

- Ask for a testimonial after good work has been done; if a customer says, "yes," then you can ask for brand referrals, too

- Ask for three referrals at the closing of a new deal

- Ask former employees for referrals; they know your business well and can speak intelligently about it (assuming they didn't leave the company for bad reasons!)

- Ask non-customers, but related professionals, for brand referrals

- Ask the best sales person you know what his/her secrets are for getting good brand referrals

- At year-end, send a hand-written thank you note to your best customers and remind them that you appreciate referrals

- Be prepared / rehearse how to ask for brand referrals — get comfortable with various techniques for asking

- Collect points for every brand referral, then reward the customer with the highest points

- Contribute to a blog on your topic, solidifying your expertise and asking for brand referrals

- Create a forwardable informative e-mail and send to your friends (in hopes that they will forward it on)

- Create a chat box for your customers on the internet / linked to your website

- Create a "friends-get-friends" campaign to expand a chain of usage

- Develop creative strategic alliances with other companies that can provide brand referrals to you (in exchange for you providing brand referrals for them)

- Do such good quality work for all customers that they will want to refer you — without you asking!

- Explain all of your various services / products so that the client is aware and can refer if the opportunity arises

- Fax press releases to existing customers and ask for brand referrals that way

(Treasure Chest of Ideas, continued)

- Free happy birthday party to the customer who brings in the most new clients

- Free trial for a new customer who is recommended by another customer

- Give customers a good trade-in deal for three successful brand references

- Give customers free samples to share with referees

- Give free product sample to referred customers

- Have customers bring in friends to try new products

- Increase value / bonus of the benefit for each higher number of referrals, e.g., one brand referral gets you X, five brand referrals gets you X + Y, 10 brand referrals gets you X + Y + Z

- Mention your brand referral scheme in your company e-mail / newsletter

- Offer a client reduced fees for services in exchange for X number of referrals

- Offer incentive / finder's fee

- Offer recognition in exchange for brand referrals

- Partner with others who have a database of customers like yours — refer each others' businesses

- Pass it on — Reward the customer when *their* referrals refer customers, too

- Place a sign in your office or on your website saying, "Referrals appreciated" and explain your finder's fee arrangement

- Provide 'talk-of-the-town' event marketing and ask participants there to share the good experience with others

- Publish articles in industry; in your byline, ask for referrals and give them an e-mail where they can reach you

- Record the success rate of all brand referrals, and reward those who brought in the most

- Recruit a high-level team of 'brand ambassadors' and offer a special privilege to them in exchange for brand referrals

- Refer other businesses to customers when those businesses provide services you don't; they will be more likely to recommend you that way

- Review customer feedback forms to find out who is most satisfied with your work; ask those individuals for brand referrals

- Reward both parties if a brand referral becomes a sale

- Reward staff members for getting brand referrals

- Send out a postcard to customers, asking for contact names and numbers of potential brand referees; include self-addressed stamped envelope for return

- Send out an SMS / text message asking for a brand referral; ask clients to forward it on

(Treasure Chest of Ideas, continued)

- Speak at a conference and ask for brand referrals at the end

- Sponsor a "brand referral party" where the price of entry for each person is to share names and contact info of five potential customers within your target market

- State in your contract that you request X referrals as part of the agreement

- Stay in touch with ex-customers; you never know — they might refer you!

- Study models for brand referrals, like multi-level marketing, e.g., Amway

- Under-promise, over-deliver — this will lead to brand referrals

- Use internet blogging to influence others and ask for brand referrals

- Use member-gets-member scheme if you run a club, organization, etc.

- Watch for referral trends — Who? What type of business? What triggered that brand referral?

- When receiving a brand referral, make an immediate thoughtful expression of gratitude

- Write up a case study that highlights the services you provide, then send it to customers and ask for a brand referral of anybody they know who might benefit from similar services

GETTING MORE CUSTOMER REFERRALS:
BRAND REFERRAL SCRIPTS THAT WORK!

Video: Session #15, time 16:13

Asking for brand referrals can be nerve-wracking, so it's no wonder that most business people avoid it. But it can be one of the most fruitful ways to get new business. After all, your current customers already know how great you are, so half the battle is won. The referred customer will be much more likely to give your brand a try because you have been recommended by someone they know.

In case you're saying to yourself, "I agree referrals are important, Brenda, but I just count on my customers to refer business to me without having to ask," trust me — that won't work. Think about it: Your customers are busy with their own businesses and lives. They probably haven't stopped to think about others they know who could benefit from what you have to offer. If you ask, however, they'll give it some thought.

How do you actually ask for a brand referral? There are several techniques, and the scripts that follow will help you. If you feel uncomfortable or nervous about asking a client for a referral, working with an outline / script at first will help you keep your nerves at bay.

Remember that it's okay if your customer says "no." If they're satisfied with your brand, most customers will be happy to help, so the occasional "no" answer is hardly a big deal. If your customer is especially open to the idea, you can also use the opportunity to ask for a testimonial as well. You can then use that testimonial on your website and other marketing materials.

Here are a few ways you can get valuable brand referrals:

Script #1 — A non-committal way of asking for referrals.

"I'm really glad that our product (service) has been valuable to you. Of course, we'd love to have more customers just like you. So, with your permission, I'd like to give you some of our (my) business cards (brochures) to pass on to anyone else who could benefit from what we (I) do. Would it be alright if I leave these with you?"

Script #2 — Another non-committal way of asking for a referral while also offering reciprocation and rewards.

"I'm really glad that our product (service) has been valuable to you. When you are talking to others who might benefit from what we do, I would appreciate you telling them about us. We always appreciate brand referrals, and of course, we're happy to refer business to you whenever we can, too. In fact, we reward our customers for referrals by offering a special gift (offer), such as _____."

Script #3 — A slightly more direct approach.

"I'm so happy to find out that our product (service) has been helpful to you. Do you know anyone else who could benefit from what we do? If so, I'd love to get their contact information from you." After receiving the names: "Would it be alright with you if I contact them directly and mention that you referred me?"

Script #4 — When you offer more than your current customer knows about.

"I'm really glad you've been pleased with my service. If you know others who might benefit from what I offer, I'd be grateful for a brand referral. In fact, you might not be aware that I also do _____. That may not be a useful service for you, specifically, but do you know someone else who might benefit from that?"

Script #5 — When your customer might not know who your ideal customer is.

"I'm really glad that you've been happy with our service (product). If you know any mid-sized law or accounting firms that need to create customized software for their practices, we'd love to be able to help them out as well. Would you have a moment to share some names and numbers with me?"

Script #6 — When you aren't absolutely certain your customer is thrilled with your brand.

"We certainly hope that you've been happy with our product (service.) If not, of course, we'd love to hear how we can improve. If so, though, we'd be very grateful if you could pass along our information to any friends, relatives, or colleagues who you believe could benefit from what we do. Would you be able to share with me some names and numbers of people I can contact?

Script #7 — When you want the customer / client to make the introduction. This approach works best with customers you know well or with whom you have worked for a considerable length of time.

"We value your business so much, and it's always such a pleasure to work with you. I was wondering if you knew anyone else who might benefit from what we do? If so, I would be very grateful if you would call him/her or send him/her an e-mail introducing us. Hearing about our brand from you will, I'm sure, make him/her feel more comfortable."

Script #8 — When your customer is resistant to giving you referrals.

After getting a "no": "Perhaps you've had bad experiences with giving referrals in the past?" After hearing your customer's objections, if the objection is about past experiences with hard-sell techniques: "I understand what you mean, and what I can tell you is that we never pester anyone to do business with us and never overstep our boundaries. If you're more comfortable with a different approach, perhaps you can send your connection an e-mail first to make sure they're open to hearing from us? Of course, I assure we would be very respectful of their time and attention."

Script #9 — When your customer is resistant to referrals after you've tried Script #8.

"I understand your discomfort with offering brand referrals, especially if you've had bad experiences in the past. I just want to say that, first of all, we don't have to use your name at all when we contact the referral, if that helps you to feel more comfortable." If you still receive a "no": "No problem. In the future, when you're speaking with someone you think might benefit from services (products) like ours, I'd be grateful if you would consider mentioning us. Thanks again for being such a great customer."

DETERMINING SUPERIORITY WORKSHEET

Paperback: Chapter 15, page 123   *Video: Session #16, time 15:25*

1. **How your products and services have *true superiority*.**

   List here the aspects of your products and/or services which are truly superior vs. competition. These should be the ways in which what you have to offer is noticeably better and, therefore, how you offer true differentiation compared to the products and services of your key competitors. Be honest with yourself! Enlist the help of others if you need help looking at your products and services with an objective eye.

   _____

   _____

   _____

   _____

   _____

   _____

2. **Your products and services that are *parity* in performance.**

   Here, list out all aspects of your products and services that are — let's face it — *equal* in performance to your key competitors' products and services. These would be areas where your customers probably wouldn't see or experience any meaningful difference when interfacing with your brand.

   _____

   _____

   _____

   _____

   _____

COMPETITIVE WEBSITE REVIEW: LIKES AND DISLIKES

Video: Session #16, time 24:39

Visit the websites of three to five of your competitors. What do you like and dislike about each one? What are you doing on your site that you feel is better than competition? What is that competitor's site doing well that you *aren't* doing on your site? What ideas could you incorporate into your own website? Remember: With all things brand-related, it's about responding to the customer's need ... which sites best respond to your customers' needs the clearest? Pay particular attention to the home page, and think of it as the front door to your office ... are you inviting the customer in similar to the way you would if that customer were standing in front of you?

Competitive Website #1: _____

What you like, and why:

What you don't like, and why:

\
\
\
\
\
\
\

Competitive Website #2: _____

What you like, and why:

What you don't like, and why:

Competitive Website #3: _____

What you like, and why: What you don't like, and why:

_____   _____

_____   _____

_____   _____

_____   _____

_____   _____

Competitive Website #4: _____

What you like, and why: What you don't like, and why:

_____   _____

_____   _____

_____   _____

_____   _____

_____   _____

Competitive Website #5: _____

What you like, and why: What you don't like, and why:

_____   _____

_____   _____

_____   _____

_____   _____

Digging Deeper Into Your Brand's Strengths & Weaknesses

Paperback: Chapter 15, page 136   *Video: Session #16, time 33:00*

Step 1*:

On the left-hand side, below and on the next page, is a list of common business strengths and weaknesses along with some blank lines underneath the list where you can add a few more. Once you've got all possible strengths and weaknesses listed there, go through and decide if each line represents a "strength" or a "weakness" for your specific brand. If it's a strength, place an "S" in the bracket to the left of the word. If it's a weakness, place a "W" in the bracket. Then, go back and circle what you believe to be the top three strengths and the top three weaknesses for your brand.

1. **Possible strengths and weaknesses of your brand:**

2. **Prove it — how do you *really* know this is a strength or a weakness?**

[   ]   Unique Positioning

[   ]   Differentiated Benefits

[   ]   Reliability / Consistency

[   ]   Ability to Respond Quickly to Market Needs

[   ]   After-Purchase Service

[   ]   Guarantees / Warranties

[   ]   Availability / Distribution

[   ]   Staff / Team Performance

[   ]   Packaging

[   ]   Labeling / Artwork

[   ]   Quality

[   ]   Value for Money

[   ]   Flexibility

[   ]   Price Point

(Continued on the next page)

[   ]   Customer Awareness   _____

[   ]   _____   _____

[   ]   _____   _____

[   ]   _____   _____

[   ]   _____   _____

[   ]   _____   _____

[   ]   _____   _____

Step 2:

For each of the top three strengths and three weaknesses that you have circled above, challenge yourself! Fill in the blank under the "Prove it" column with the rationale for your choices. How do you *know* your three biggest strengths are truly strengths? How would you prove it? Likewise for your weaknesses, how do you *know* that what you perceive to be your top three weaknesses are indeed the biggest ones in your customers' eyes? What is the evidence for that? And, for both strengths and weaknesses, how compelling is the evidence?

** GROUP VERSION **

*You can also do this exercise in a group. Here are the instructions:

For Step 1:

Grab some friends, colleagues, staff members, customers, and/or other connections — all who know your brand well — and ask them to help out. Purchase some "power dots" — a set of small, round stickers of two distinctly different colors (red and blue, for example). Let the blue color represent strengths and the red color represent weaknesses. Then, take a stack of blank papers, and write one attribute on its own sheet until each possible attribute has been written on a separate piece of paper. Tape up each piece of paper next to each other on a wall. Each member involved in this exercise then gets three red dots and three blue dots. Each person places one blue dot on each of the three attributes of your brand that they believe to be the strongest. Likewise, each person will place one red dot on each of the three attributes of your brand that they believe to be the weakest. Assess the results together.

For Step 2:

Now, you and the group can share collectively the evidence you all believe proves these strengths and weaknesses to be true. Inevitably, some good, meaty, and strategic discussions will come of this! And, you — as your business owner — will learn a lot from others' perspectives, too.

What's Important to Your Customers?

Paperback: Chapter 15, page 136   *Video: Session #16, time 34:08*

On the left-hand side, below, **circle the strengths** and **underline the weaknesses** that you've already identified for your own business and brand (again, feel free to use the spaces at the bottom of the column to add your own, if you have others). Once you've done that, ignore that list for a minute, and shift to reviewing the full list of possible brand attributes on the right-hand side of the page. Assess this list *from the perspective of your customers.* Go line-by-line through each of these attributes again, and consider which three your customers think are *most* important. Now, reflect on which three are *least* important to customers. (If you are not sure, ask some of your most trusted customers to complete this form for you!)

Once that's done, look back at the strengths and weaknesses that you circled and underlined on the left-hand column. Do your brand's strongest attributes match up with what your customers care about most? Or, are your strongest attributes those which are not that important to your customers?

1. Identified strengths and weaknesses of your brand:	2. Which ones are most important to your customers?
Unique Positioning	Unique Positioning
Differentiated Benefits	Differentiated Benefits
Reliability / Consistency	Reliability / Consistency
Ability to Respond Quickly to Market Needs	Ability to Respond Quickly to Market Needs
After-Purchase Service	After-Purchase Service
Guarantees / Warranties	Guarantees / Warranties
Availability / Distribution	Availability / Distribution
Staff / Team Performance	Staff / Team Performance
Packaging	Packaging
Labeling / Artwork	Labeling / Artwork
Quality	Quality
Value for Money	Value for Money
Flexibility	Flexibility
Price Point	Price Point
Customer Awareness	Customer Awareness
_____	_____
_____	_____
_____	_____

GROWING YOUR TEAM WORKSHEET:
YOUR "TEAM" IS BIGGER THAN YOU THINK!

Paperback: Chapter 16, page 139   *Video: Session #17, time 01:31*

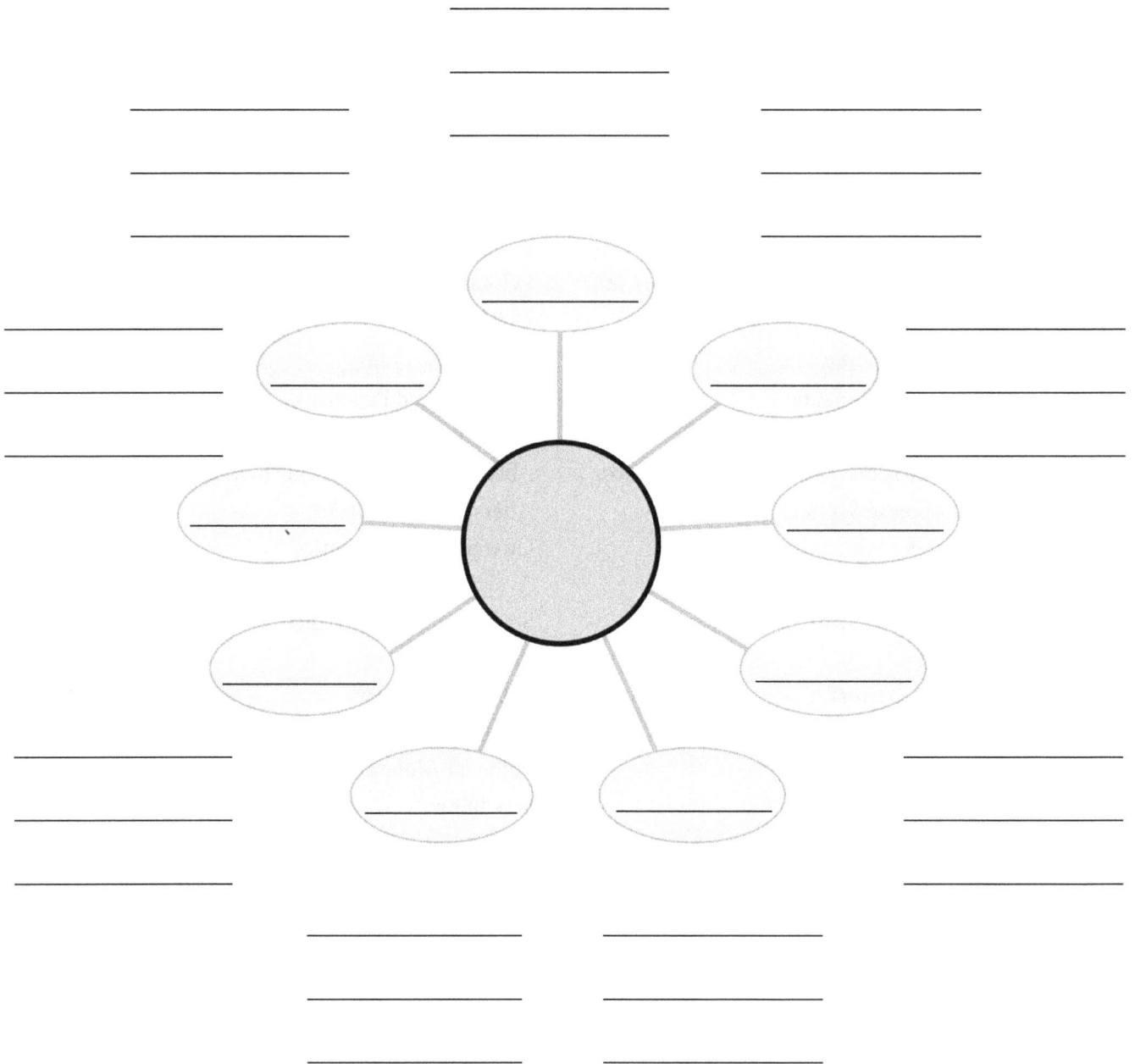

GROWING YOUR TEAM MASTER LIST OF CATEGORIES: TREASURE CHEST OF IDEAS

Video: Session #17, time 03:08

Below is a compiled list of possible Team members who could help you build your brand. Use this as a thought-starter … who else do you know that could be part of your extended "marketing team?"

Possible Team Members from Your Professional Life:

- Current staff
- Previous staff members
- Existing customers
- Directors of your company
- Shareholders / stakeholders
- Strategic partners / alliance partners
- Twitter followers
- Facebook fans
- LinkedIn connections
- Vendors / suppliers
- Consultants
- Other entrepreneurs
- Members of your mastermind group
- Advisors
- Advertisers
- Professional clubs / Associations
- People met at networking events
- Reporters
- TV reporters
- Lawyers
- Accountants
- Auditors
- Bankers
- Brokers
- Advertising agencies
- Public relations representatives
- Copywriters / editors

- Designers
- Social media / Internet experts
- Researchers
- Landlords / realtors
- Insurers
- Loss adjusters
- Printers
- Messengers / delivery people
- Mail carriers
- Publishers
- Guards
- Drivers
- Movers
- Secretaries
- Receptionists
- Surveyors / project managers
- Trade delegations
- Industry leaders
- Regulators
- International organizations
- Franchisees
- Government bodies
- Government officials
- Radio DJs
- TV show hosts
- Embassy officials

(Treasure Chest of Ideas, continued)

Possible Team Members from Your Personal Life:

- Significant other
- Adult children
- Nuclear family members (sisters, brothers, parents ...)
- Extended family members (aunts, uncles, cousins, nieces, nephews ...)
- Friends
- Team members' families and friends
- Social clubs / Associations / Country clubs
- Acquaintances
- Alumni
- Conference participants
- Teachers
- Doctors
- Dentists
- Charities you're involved with
- Helpers / House cleaners
- Attendants
- Event planners / organizers
- Sports personalities
- High School buddies
- College roommates
- Sorority / Fraternity mates from the past

ELEVATOR BRAND INTRODUCTION

Paperback: Chapter 16, page 140   *Video: Session #17, time 06:21*

You have no doubt heard of an "elevator speech." Well, I like to think of it as an "elevator brand introduction."

Imagine this: You enter an elevator on the 20th floor and press "G" for the ground floor. As the elevator descends to the 19th floor, it stops, and a man gets on and says, "Hello." You think he could be an interesting business prospect. At best, you have about 20 seconds to speak and introduce your brand. What are you going to say?

I personally learned the hard way about not being prepared for this kind of situation. It was 2008, and I had just launched my first book. In fact, the book had just been released two or three days before. I was at an author's convention and was carrying a copy of my book around with me. I got into an elevator, someone bumped into me, and the book fell out of my arms and onto the floor. A woman bent down, picked up the book, looked at the cover, and said, "Wow! Interesting title. Whose is this?" as she looked around the packed elevator. One glance at the woman, and I instantly realized who she was — the head of a major publishing company!

"It's mine," I replied.

Turning to look straight at me, she said, "Tell me more."

I was dumbstruck! I hadn't had time to think about my elevator brand introduction, and here I was facing this incredible opportunity! I remember fumbling through a general statement — I'm sure it wasn't particularly eloquent — and unfortunately, nothing ever came of it.

Tough lesson learned! You can bet I've never let that happen again. I sat down right away and perfected my elevator brand introduction for that particular book brand.

You never know what could come from an opportunity like this, so make sure you're prepared. Being ready with a concise and meaningful way to describe your brand is key.

Taking Your Brand Introduction on the Road

This type of brand introduction isn't only for elevators, of course. Think about the first question someone usually asks when you meet them: "What do you do?" If you don't have a fast, engaging, crystal clear answer that communicates your brand, you've missed out on a potential chance to bring another marketing member onto your team.

ELEVATOR BRAND INTRODUCTION: TOP 10 TIPS

Video: Session #17, time 04:46

Here are the top 10 most important points to remember when creating your elevator brand introduction:

1. Keep your elevator brand intro short and concise — 20 seconds or less is best.

2. Don't just state your "job title"; describe what you do in a compelling way. "I'm an accountant" doesn't do much for your brand; in fact, it makes you sound just like everyone else — and that's no way to stand out in a crowd!

3. Describe *who* you do it for. Who are your customers / Target Group?

4. In your opening sentence (to grab the person's attention), describe the value, benefit, and quality that you bring to your customers in quantifiable terms — i.e., don't just say that you help your clients grow their businesses; say that you have helped X number of clients grow their businesses by XX% in a 12-month period. In other words, offer an example of what you have done for one or more customers.

5. Try to include information that will differentiate your brand from your competition. Using your Brand Positioning Statement, focus on the Benefits section. That's most likely where the potential customer will be interested. Remember, they want to know what's in it for them!

6. Don't use industry jargon in case the other person is unaware of the "lingo," and avoid vague words and long sentences. Keep it snappy, short, and concise.

7. After you have described what you do and for whom, ask the person a question that requires more than just a "yes" or "no" answer to stimulate further conversation. For example, don't say: "Is tax analysis important for your business?" (The only possible answer is either "yes" or "no.") Instead say, "How important is tax analysis to your business?" (There is a wide range of answers available to this question!)

8. Keep it conversational, and be careful not to sound like a salesperson.

9. Always end by asking if you can contact the person to talk about their needs further or set up a meeting. If this person's business isn't a great target for your brand, give him or her a couple of extra business cards and ask them to share those cards with anybody they think would benefit from your services.

10. Practice your elevator brand intro until it rolls off your tongue and is so natural to you that you could repeat it in your sleep. Be careful that it doesn't sound rehearsed, though. Ask a friend or colleague to listen to it to make sure you don't sound like you've memorized it.

Examples:

Here are some sample elevator brand introductions:

- "I help families save money so that the kids can go to university and the parents can enjoy their retirement. I'm happy to say that my insurance and financial planning services have saved customers thousands of dollars annually. How about you — do you have children? …

How many?" After receiving the answer: "I'd love to set up a time to talk with you about how I could help you pay for your children's education and still have money to retire. How helpful would that be to you?"

- "At ACME Printing, we help companies save time and reduce costs by up to 15% through making it easier to print invoices and accounts receivable forms, and to process payroll checks. What's most important to *your* business when it comes to printing requirements?" After receiving the answer: "I feel confident we could help you save money on printing. Could I get your card? When would be a good time to contact you to talk about how we could help you solve these issues?"

- "I help women look and feel their best by providing them with the top-rated cosmetics in the industry and showing them how to apply those cosmetics well. How about you — which of your current cosmetics are you least satisfied with?" After receiving the answer: "We have a terrific lipstick that lasts all day. I'd love to show it to you. When could we get together so that you could try it yourself?"

- "We've created a brand of software that allows you to track the return on investment of all of your marketing efforts in one database — from print to television and radio to Internet to SMS to billboards. No more lost revenues on marketing efforts that don't work. What kind of marketing methods does your company use?" After receiving the answer: "I definitely see how we could help your marketing become more efficient and cost-effective. Let me send you some information via e-mail. After you've reviewed it, I'd be happy to show you how we can help you bring in more business for less money."

- "I run my own human relations consulting business for SMEs, saving them an annual average of $329 per employee and helping them keep their employees for longer periods of time. What's your biggest issue with regard to employee hiring and retention?" After receiving the answer: "I've got some proven strategies for solving challenges like that. If you'd like, we could set up a time to meet up and talk about how I could help you apply those strategies to your specific circumstances."

Creating Your Elevator Brand Introduction

As you sit down to write your own brand introduction, start by thinking about the benefits your brand provides your customers. Remember that the person you're talking with is interested in how you can help him or her. Awards and accolades (your Reasons Why) may be impressive, but they don't offer a tangible, quantifiable benefit.

Make note of what you've delivered to your current customers, and use these in your elevator brand introduction if at all possible. Use this quantifiable information in your opening sentence in order to grab the listener's attention.

Be prepared for different answers to your open-ended question. Know your products and services inside and out so that you can spontaneously adjust your answer to the needs of the individual you're talking with.

Finally, test your brand intro to make sure you won't get a "So what?" response. Is it exciting enough? Have you shown exactly what you can do? Do you deliver it with passion? How will what you've said directly build the brand image you are working toward?

KNOW YOUR COMPETITION WORKSHEET

Paperback: Chapter 17, page 152   *Video: Session #18, time 02:31*

Knowing your competition well is just as fundamental to building a good business as is focusing on your own brand growth. After all, if you don't know who you're competing against, how can you set a strategy to win?

Smart brand builders put time and effort into getting to know their competitors. Here are some exercises and questions you can ask yourself to increase the knowledge of your key competitors. Begin by listing out your most important competitors and then answer the questions for each one:

Competitor's Name: _____

a. Find two the three things this competitor is doing *right*. What competitive advantages do they have? Consider positioning, products, services, quality, price/performance ratio, ability to respond to market needs, customer service, geographic coverage, production and technical capabilities, marketing, Internet presence, operations, distribution, sales, research, employees, HR policies, financing structure, etc. List these advantages here.

_____

_____

_____

b. Now, brainstorm ways you could do these particular things *better*. (Remember the paperclip challenge, and don't fall prey to the "We can't" mentality …)

_____

_____

_____

c. Write down three critical pieces of information you *don't* have about this competitor that — if you did — would make a significant difference to your ability to strengthen and build your own brand:

_____

_____

_____

d. Now, think about it … in what (legal and ethical) ways could you get access to that information? Brainstorm here:

_____

_____

_____

e. Once you know this competitor better, what products or services could you provide to this competitor's customers to interest them in your brand? What marketing activities could you implement to reach this brand's core target group?

_____

_____

_____

_____

How to Find Out What Competitors Are Doing Right: Treasure Chest of Ideas

Video: Session #18, time 02:34

Based on past *Smarter Branding* workshops from around the globe, below is a compiled list of some possible ways you can find out more about what your competitors are doing *right*. Knowing that helps you set your own brand's course in what can often be tricky competitive waters. Use this list as a thought-starter, then think: What else could you do — given your particular industry and business — to find out what your competitors are doing well?

- Analyze information on competitors' packaging
- Analyze marketing materials / advertisements
- Ask an agency / vendor how / what competitors are doing
- Ask customers about competitive products and services, what they like and don't like
- Ask friends and family who use competitors' products / services
- Ask headhunters what they know about competitors
- Ask members of the press what they know
- Ask target group members to compare and contrast our products / services vs. competitors'
- Ask team members in other markets to share what that competitor is doing there
- Ask vendors what they like about working with certain competitors
- Ask your staff if they know someone who works with a competitor or used to work there
- Attend a competitor's workshop / activity / press conference / conference / product launch
- Buy a product from your competitor and observe their purchasing process
- Buy competitors' products / use or try their services
- Call clients who also use a particular competitor, and ask them questions
- Call clients who hired your competition to understand what drove that decision
- Call a competitor's hotline and complain to see how the situation is handled
- Commission a third party survey about the competitor
- Compare loyalty programs
- Compare published data / results (industry averages vs. your own results, for example)
- Conduct a homemade focus group using competitor's products

(Treasure Chest of Ideas, continued)

- Conduct a consumer survey to understand competitive strengths

- Conduct online key word analysis on your competitors' websites

- Conduct online search for information about competitors

- Conduct tests on competitors' products

- Get to know a competitor's suppliers (materials and equipment)

- Have an offsite day where you benchmark competitors' products, services, and advertising / promotions

- Interview friendly competitors

- Interview partners who used to work with competitors

- Interview salespeople out in the field — what are they seeing?

- Issue a questionnaire to your customers about your competitor's products

- Join associations / clubs to which key competitors belong

- Monitor investment activities of competitors

- Monitor patent applications and business changes

- Read related trade publications

- Review annual reports / brochures of competitors

- Review available financial analysis (if competitor is a public company)

- Review competitors' social media sites

- Review every page of your competitors' websites

- See what market research on competitors is available

- See what competitors do in-store / where their products are being sold

- See with what companies competitors are affiliated

- Set up Google Alerts for key competitors' names and key officers

- Subscribe to any competitors' newsletters

- Subscribe to competitors' RSS feeds

- Track any research that competitors publish

- Use a news clipping service or assign the task to a team member

- Visit competitors' booths at an exhibit and ask questions

- Visit competitors' chatrooms online

INFERRED COMPETITOR BRAND POSITIONING STATEMENT WORKSHEET

Paperback: Chapter 17, page 155   *Video: Session #18, time 11:17*

TO *(Competitor's Target Group):*

- *Demographics, Psychographics, Attitudes*

- *Current Usage & Behaviors*

- *Needs (Functional / Emotional)*

(COMPETITOR'S BRAND NAME) _____

IS THE BRAND OF *(Competitive Framework):* _____

_____

(Competing mainly with) _____

_____

THAT PROVIDES *(Competitor's Benefits):* _____

_____

_____

BECAUSE *(Competitor's Reasons Why):*

1. _____

2. _____

3. _____

THE BRAND CHARACTER OF THIS COMPETITOR IS:

(Descriptors and/or Narrative) _____

_____

_____

Comparison: Your Brand Positioning Statement vs. Key Competitors

Paperback: Chapter 17, page 157   *Video: Session #18, time 11:24*

Once you've inferred your key competitor's Brand Positioning Statement ("BPS") based on thorough competitive analysis, insert into the format on page 56 each individual element of (a) your own BPS, and (b) that of a key competitor. (You can do a separate sheet for each of your key competitors.) This kind of side-by-side analysis allows you to see where the two brands are most similar and most different.

Here are questions to consider as you review the two Positioning Statements:

- Do you and this competitor have similar or different targets?

- How different are your target group's functional and emotional needs?

- Do you fill a need that your competitor doesn't?

- OR, does this competitor's brand fill a need that your brand doesn't?

- Who does this competitor believe are "its" competitors? (Is *your* brand on this competitor's radar?)

- What benefits does this competitor offer that are similar or different from yours?

- What benefits can your brand own that this competitor can't?

- Do you promote that particular benefit enough?

- What reasons why does your competitor use, and are they stronger or weaker than yours?

- If you were someone in your target group, which brand would you want to buy solely based on the reasons why?

- How does this competitor's brand character speak to its target market?

- How does this competitor's brand character compare to yours?

	Your Own Brand Positioning Elements	Your Competitor's Brand Positioning Elements
Brand Name:		
Target Group:		
Demographics		
Psychographics		
Attitudes		
Current Usage		
Behaviors		
Needs:		
Functional		
Emotional		
Competitive Framework:		
Is the Brand of		
Competing mainly with		
Benefits:		
That provides		
Reasons Why:	• • •	• • •
Brand Character:		
Descriptors or Narrative		

IMPLEMENTING LEARNING FOR YOUR BRAND:
FINALIZING YOUR TOP 10 BRAND-BUILDING IDEAS

Paperback: Chapter 18, page 161   *Video: Session #19, time 04:13*

List your top <u>20</u> potential ideas here (the ideas you 'starred' on the Ideas & Actions Template). No need to prioritize them yet — just write down what you believe to be your 20 biggest brand-building ideas:

- _____
- _____
- _____
- _____
- _____
- _____
- _____
- _____
- _____
- _____
- _____
- _____
- _____
- _____
- _____
- _____

(Continued on the next page)

- _____
- _____
- _____

Now, using the following criteria, circle the top 10 ideas which you believe are the best ones to start with.

Idea Selection Criteria

1. Fast forward to having implemented this idea … what would the outcomes be if you implemented this idea successfully?

2. How sure are you of success with this idea? What are the risks? What could go wrong or is less in your control about each idea?

3. Which of these ideas would make the biggest amount of impact on the business in the shortest amount of time? (e.g., which ones are 'low-hanging fruit?')

4. Which activities best address your customer's most important unmet needs?

5. Which activities best help eliminate your brand's weaknesses and leverage its strengths?

Now, list the top 10 ideas that you circled here. These serve as the foundation for your Action and Accountability Grid.

Top 10 Brand-Building Ideas:

- _____
- _____
- _____
- _____
- _____
- _____
- _____
- _____
- _____
- _____

ACTION AND ACCOUNTABILITY GRID:
LIGHTS, CAMERA ... ACTION!

Paperback: Chapter 18, page 161   *Video: Session #19, time 05:49*

Activity	By When	Success Looks Like ...	Who is Responsible	Sponsor / Accountability Buddy

ACTION AND ACCOUNTABILITY GRID EXAMPLE:
LIGHTS, CAMERA ... ACTION!

Paperback: Chapter 18, page 161   *Video: Session #19, time 06:59*

Activity	By When	Success Looks Like ...	Who is Responsible	Sponsor/ Accountability Buddy
1. Send hand-written "thank you" letters to long-term clients — ask how we can do better	May 30	• Response back from 80% of clients • Prompt follow up on their feedback	Sarah T.	John B.
2. Improve e-mail signature to include brand benefits and reasons why, as well as updates on new promotions	April 15	• Enquiries for additional products and services as a result of e-mail communications increase by 15%	Me	Alfred C.
3. Sign up for Google Alerts for both our brand and key competitors	April 15	• Improved industry knowledge • Improved competitive information	Robert L.	Sarah T.
4. Implement incentive payment program to encourage client brand referrals	June 30	• Incentive payment program in place and communicated to staff and clients • Obtain three referrals from clients per staff member	John B.	Susan P.
5. Write column in local newspaper about core category topics	May 30	• Printed column in newspaper once every quarter starting in June • At least three new clients per year from having read my column	Me	Alfred C.

Suggested Books

Competitive Positioning: Best Practices for Creating Brand Loyalty, Richard D. Czerniawski & Michael W. Maloney, 2011

The 22 Immutable Laws of Branding, Al Ries and Laura Ries, 2002

Brand Warfare, David D'Alessandro, 2001

How YOU™ are like Shampoo, Brenda Bence, 2008

Rising Tide: Lessons from 165 Years of Brand Building at Procter & Gamble, Davis Dyer, Frederick Dalzell, and Rowena Olegario, 2004

Emotional Branding : How Successful Brands Gain the Irrational Edge, Daryl Travis, 2000

B2B Brand Management, Philip Kotler and Waldemar Pfoertsch, 2006

ABOUT THE AUTHOR

Brenda S. Bence is Founder and President of BDA (Brand Development Associates) International Ltd., a firm that specializes in helping companies and individual clients around the world build successful, growth-oriented corporate and personal brands. As a Certified Speaking Professional, Certified Executive Coach, and dynamic trainer and consultant, Brenda has worked with hundreds of executives, managers, and entrepreneurs around the world to help them define and communicate their corporate and personal brands. Brenda spends the majority of the year traveling to present her unique approach to branding at conferences, conventions, and corporations all across the globe.

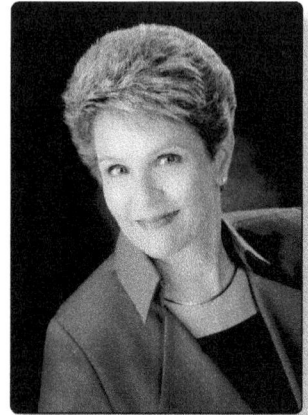

Having earned her MBA from Harvard Business School, Brenda began her career as a marketer at Procter & Gamble, first at P&G's world headquarters in the U.S., then with P&G in Europe and in Asia. She subsequently held the position of Vice President International Marketing for Bristol-Myers Squibb's consumer division, Mead Johnson, where Brenda was responsible for multiple brands across almost 50 countries.

During her 25-year career, Brenda has helped manage dozens of well-known brands, including Pantene, Vidal Sassoon Shampoo & Styling products, Head & Shoulders, Enfamil, Choc-o-Milk, and Ariel and Cheer Laundry Detergents, just to name a few.

Happily married to her husband, Daniel, Brenda splits her time between homes in Singapore and the U.S. She also sits on a number of boards of public and private companies and not-for-profit organizations. See www.BrendaBence.com.

NOTES